A First Look at Trolls

by Emma Carlson-Berne

BUMBA BOOKS™

LERNER PUBLICATIONS ◆ MINNEAPOLIS

To Finn

Note to Educators

Throughout this book, you'll find critical-thinking questions. These can be used to engage young readers in thinking critically about the topic and in using the text and photos to do so.

Lerner Publications Company
An imprint of Lerner Publishing Group, Inc.
241 First Avenue North
Minneapolis, MN 55401 USA

For reading levels and more information, look up this title at www.lernerbooks.com.

Main body text set in Helvetica Textbook Com Roman.
Typeface provided by Linotype AG.

Designer: Lauren Cooper
Lerner team: Martha Kranes

Library of Congress Cataloging-in-Publication Data

Names: Carlson-Berne, Emma, author.
Title: A first look at trolls / Emma Carlson-Berne.
Description: Minneapolis : Lerner Publications, [2021] | Series: Bumba books—fantastic creatures | Includes bibliographical references and index. | Audience: Ages 4–7 | Audience: Grades K–1 | Summary: "Beginning readers will delight in learning about trolls and the stories we tell about them. Reading is supported by close text-to-image match and carefully leveled text."— Provided by publisher.
Identifiers: LCCN 2019043141 (print) | LCCN 2019043142 (ebook) | ISBN 9781541596849 (library binding) | ISBN 9781541599765 (ebook)
Subjects: LCSH: Trolls—Juvenile literature.
Classification: LCC GR555 .B48 2021 (print) | LCC GR555 (ebook) | DDC 398.21—dc23

LC record available at https://lccn.loc.gov/2019043141
LC ebook record available at https://lccn.loc.gov/2019043142

Manufactured in the United States of America
1-47790-48230-11/13/2019

Table of Contents

Trolls!

What is that creature? It is very big and ugly. It must be a troll!

Trolls are imaginary. But people have told stories about them for a long time.

Trolls are giants in some stories. They live in forests or on mountains. They throw boulders when they are angry.

In other stories, trolls are little. They live in caves. They might try to trick people.

Where else might a troll live?

People imagine trolls have big ears and hairy feet. A troll might have long, dirty hair.

What clothing might a troll wear?

People tell stories about trolls who live under bridges. The trolls ask people riddles.

Stories say that trolls are afraid of lightning. They hide during thunderstorms.

What else might scare trolls away?

Trolls also don't like sunlight. In some stories, trolls turn to stone in the sun.

Trolls are fun to imagine!

Troll Diagram

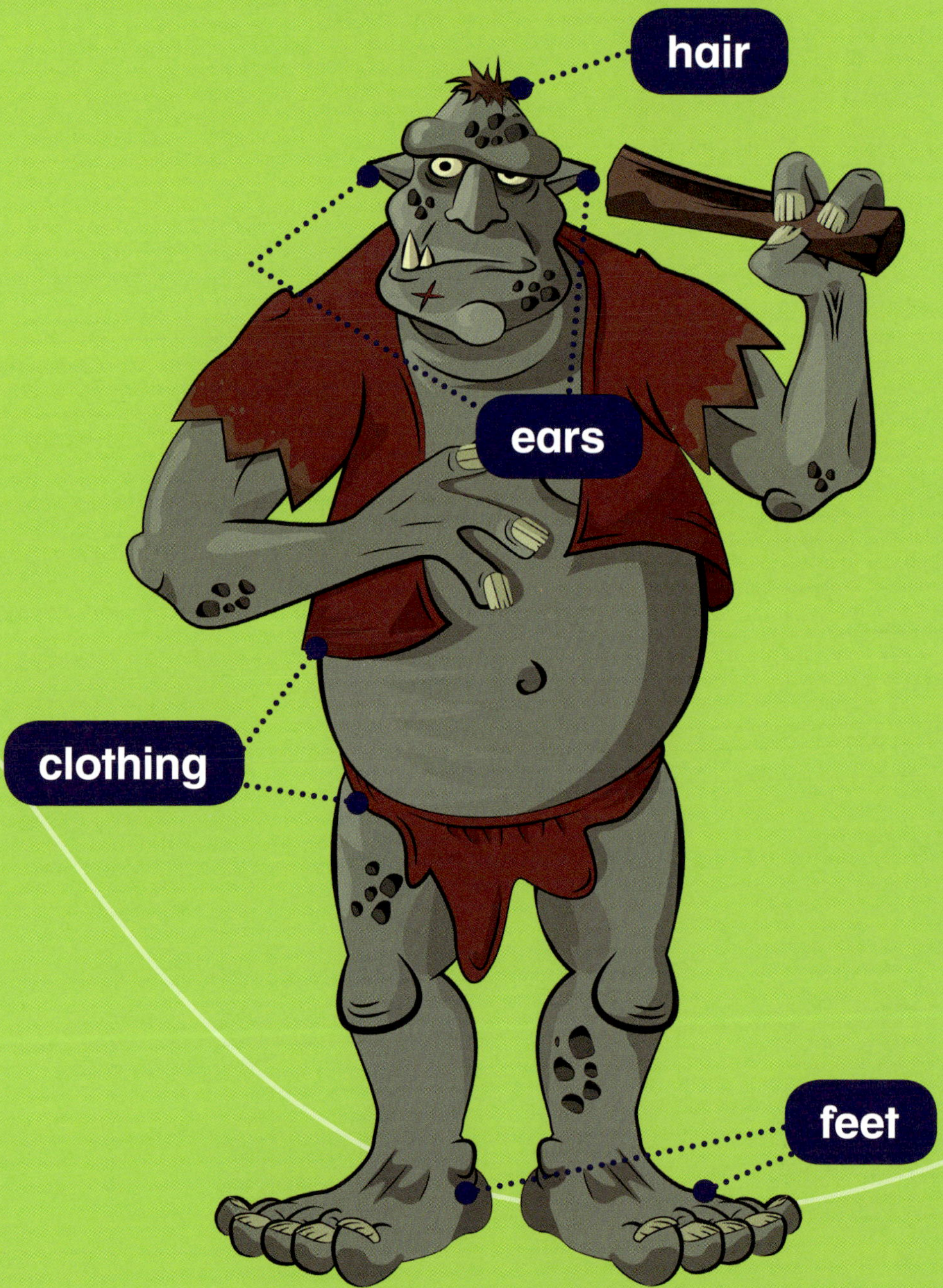

Picture Glossary

boulders

huge rocks

giants

made-up creatures who look like people but are much bigger

imaginary

something that is make-believe

riddles

puzzling questions

Read More

Beth, Georgia. *World's Best (and Worst) Riddles*. Minneapolis: Lerner Publications, 2018.

Carlson-Berne, Emma. *A First Look at Monsters*. Minneapolis: Lerner Publications, 2021.

Peters, Katie. *When Lightning Strikes*. Minneapolis: Lerner Publications, 2020.

Index

Photo Credits

Image credits: e71lena/Getty Images, p. 5; Kisa_Markiza/Getty Images, pp. 7, 23 (bottom left); Vorobiov Oleksii 8/Shutterstock.com, p. 8; John Bauer/Wikipedia Commons PD, pp. 11, 12; nomeko/Shutterstock.com, pp. 15, 23 (bottom right); Magnus Bengtsson/EyeEm/Getty Images, p. 16; Pam Susemiehl/Getty Images, p. 19; PeopleImages/Getty Images, p. 20; Gal_Istvan/Getty Images, p. 22; Miki Pavlovikj/Shutterstock.com, p. 23 (top right); Andrew Merry/Getty Images, p. 23 (top left).

Cover: Kate Smith/Getty Images (troll); ratpack223/Getty Images (background).